HowExpert

How To

Your Step By Step Guide To Fly Fishing

HowExpert with Lloyd Bentley

Copyright HowExpert™
www.HowExpert.com

For more tips related to this topic, visit HowExpert.com/flyfish.

Recommended Resources

- HowExpert.com – Quick 'How To' Guides on All Topics from A to Z by Everyday Experts.
- HowExpert.com/free – Free HowExpert Email Newsletter.
- HowExpert.com/books – HowExpert Books
- HowExpert.com/courses – HowExpert Courses
- HowExpert.com/clothing – HowExpert Clothing
- HowExpert.com/membership – HowExpert Membership Site
- HowExpert.com/affiliates – HowExpert Affiliate Program
- HowExpert.com/writers – Write About Your #1 Passion/Knowledge/Expertise & Become a HowExpert Author.
- HowExpert.com/resources – Additional HowExpert Recommended Resources
- YouTube.com/HowExpert – Subscribe to HowExpert YouTube.
- Instagram.com/HowExpert – Follow HowExpert on Instagram.
- Facebook.com/HowExpert – Follow HowExpert on Facebook.

COPYRIGHT, LEGAL NOTICE AND DISCLAIMER:

COPYRIGHT © BY HOWEXPERT™ (OWNED BY HOT METHODS). ALL RIGHTS RESERVED WORLDWIDE. NO PART OF THIS PUBLICATION MAY BE REPRODUCED IN ANY FORM OR BY ANY MEANS, INCLUDING SCANNING, PHOTOCOPYING, OR OTHERWISE WITHOUT PRIOR WRITTEN PERMISSION OF THE COPYRIGHT HOLDER.

DISCLAIMER AND TERMS OF USE: PLEASE NOTE THAT MUCH OF THIS PUBLICATION IS BASED ON PERSONAL EXPERIENCE AND ANECDOTAL EVIDENCE. ALTHOUGH THE AUTHOR AND PUBLISHER HAVE MADE EVERY REASONABLE ATTEMPT TO ACHIEVE COMPLETE ACCURACY OF THE CONTENT IN THIS GUIDE, THEY ASSUME NO RESPONSIBILITY FOR ERRORS OR OMISSIONS. ALSO, YOU SHOULD USE THIS INFORMATION AS YOU SEE FIT, AND AT YOUR OWN RISK. YOUR PARTICULAR SITUATION MAY NOT BE EXACTLY SUITED TO THE EXAMPLES ILLUSTRATED HERE; IN FACT, IT'S LIKELY THAT THEY WON'T BE THE SAME, AND YOU SHOULD ADJUST YOUR USE OF THE INFORMATION AND RECOMMENDATIONS ACCORDINGLY.

THE AUTHOR AND PUBLISHER DO NOT WARRANT THE PERFORMANCE, EFFECTIVENESS OR APPLICABILITY OF ANY SITES LISTED OR LINKED TO IN THIS BOOK. ALL LINKS ARE FOR INFORMATION PURPOSES ONLY AND ARE NOT WARRANTED FOR CONTENT, ACCURACY OR ANY OTHER IMPLIED OR EXPLICIT PURPOSE.

ANY TRADEMARKS, SERVICE MARKS, PRODUCT NAMES OR NAMED FEATURES ARE ASSUMED TO BE THE PROPERTY OF THEIR RESPECTIVE OWNERS, AND ARE USED ONLY FOR REFERENCE. THERE IS NO IMPLIED ENDORSEMENT IF WE USE ONE OF THESE TERMS.

NO PART OF THIS BOOK MAY BE REPRODUCED, STORED IN A RETRIEVAL SYSTEM, OR TRANSMITTED BY ANY OTHER MEANS: ELECTRONIC, MECHANICAL, PHOTOCOPYING, RECORDING, OR OTHERWISE, WITHOUT THE PRIOR WRITTEN PERMISSION OF THE AUTHOR.

ANY VIOLATION BY STEALING THIS BOOK OR DOWNLOADING OR SHARING IT ILLEGALLY WILL BE PROSECUTED BY LAWYERS TO THE FULLEST EXTENT. THIS PUBLICATION IS PROTECTED UNDER THE US COPYRIGHT ACT OF 1976 AND ALL OTHER APPLICABLE INTERNATIONAL, FEDERAL, STATE AND LOCAL LAWS AND ALL RIGHTS ARE RESERVED, INCLUDING RESALE RIGHTS: YOU ARE NOT ALLOWED TO GIVE OR SELL THIS GUIDE TO ANYONE ELSE.

THIS PUBLICATION IS DESIGNED TO PROVIDE ACCURATE AND AUTHORITATIVE INFORMATION WITH REGARD TO THE SUBJECT MATTER COVERED. IT IS SOLD WITH THE UNDERSTANDING THAT THE AUTHORS AND PUBLISHERS ARE NOT ENGAGED IN RENDERING LEGAL, FINANCIAL, OR OTHER PROFESSIONAL ADVICE. LAWS AND PRACTICES OFTEN VARY FROM STATE TO STATE AND IF LEGAL OR OTHER EXPERT ASSISTANCE IS REQUIRED, THE SERVICES OF A PROFESSIONAL SHOULD BE SOUGHT. THE AUTHORS AND PUBLISHER SPECIFICALLY DISCLAIM ANY LIABILITY THAT IS INCURRED FROM THE USE OR APPLICATION OF THE CONTENTS OF THIS BOOK.

COPYRIGHT BY HOWEXPERT™ (OWNED BY HOT METHODS)
ALL RIGHTS RESERVED WORLDWIDE.

Table of Contents

Recommended Resources 2

Chapter 1: Introduction 6

Chapter 2: Reel, Rod, Backing, Line and Leader 10

The Reel 13

The Rod 16

The Backing 20

The Fly Line 21

The Leader 23

Chapter 3: Flies, Flies and Tying Flies 28

Chapter 4: Tools of the Fly Fisher's Trade ... 33

Chapter 5: Footwear and Waders 36

Chapter 6: The Waters We Fish 39

Chapter 7: The Fish 47

Chapter 8: Let's Go Fishing! 55

Chapter 9: Casting 66

Chapter 10: Hooking Up and Playing 84

Chapter 11 – Landing and Releasing the Fish 94

Chapter 12: When to Fly fish 99

Chapter 13: Where to Fly fish 106

Chapter 14: Guides and Drift Boats 109

Chapter 15: More Instruction and More Gear 113

Chapter 16: Putting It All Together: A Day on the River 117

About the Expert 127

Recommended Resources 128

Chapter 1: Introduction

This book will get you started in the sport of fly fishing. It touches on the basic methods, gear and strategies you'll need to start casting a fly to a fish. There are many advanced areas that we'll skim over or ignore completely in this lesson. Fly fishing is an age-old tree of tradition and knowledge, with deep roots and thousands of branches. Reading this book will give you a good sense of the tree itself. For simplicity, we'll stick to some of the most popular forms and features of this incredibly rewarding pastime.

We'll fish on moving water: rivers, creeks and streams. Once you can fly fish moving water, still water-fishing, on lakes, for instance, follows quite naturally.

A BROWN TROUT IN OCTOBER ON THE BOW RIVER NEAR CANMORE, ALBERTA, CANADA

We'll focus on fishing the dry fly, which floats on top of the water. It resembles a flying insect that is recognizable to fish as a food source. You cast out the dry fly; it lands and floats down the stream before your eyes. Then, if you are lucky, you'll witness the spectacle of a fish rising to inspect and perhaps take the fly from the surface.

A DRY FLY CALLED THE "TURK'S TARANTULA" – AN ATTRACTOR PATTERN

Dry fly fishing is considered the most rewarding and classic form of fly fishing, and has been so for more than three hundred years. Other flies, such as nymphs, leeches and streamers, are fished to sink down to where the fish are. Dry flies are fished to entice the fish up to the surface of the water.

We will home in on waters that contain primarily trout, a cold water fish, and the ultimate challenge for most fly fishers. All species of trout are found in most northern hemispheres, and even some southern ones, such as New Zealand, which boasts some of the finest brown-trout fishing in the world.

Because both men and women participate in fly fishing, "fly fisher" is the term we will use when referring to the individual fly fishing student.

FISH ON! THE JACKPINE RIVER IN NORTHERN ONTARIO, CANADA

We practice "catch and release" in this book, and on the river. This means putting all caught fish back into the water alive and well. Fresh fish can be enjoyed from the supermarket. Fly fishing is about more than a meal; it is about taking up a great hobby, perfecting a skill and matching wits with a worthy opponent.

You may get hooked on fly fishing. It offers drama, suspense, adventures in nature and jolts of adrenalin. You may have to miss work or appointments. You may find, too, that this book reaches beyond fly fishing and into the realms of science, art and, even, philosophy. Because this is a sport of both mind and matter, these forays are unavoidable.

Fly fishing should be studied in stages, which, much like learning music, include both theory and practice. You will read books like this one, and follow your interest to other sources, including magazines and manuals. You will learn how to tie knots and cast a fly, and you practice.

You will also learn how to stroll along a river bank, flipping over rocks to find bugs, studying the flow of currents, and listening to the nuanced sounds of moving water. You will need to know something about insects and weather, seasons and spawning cycles and, eventually, the phases of the moon. Let's start by learning how to cast the fly upon the water.

EARLY SPRING ON THE CROWSNEST RIVER IN SOUTHERN ALBERTA, CANADA

Chapter 2: Reel, Rod, Backing, Line and Leader

In the sport of fly fishing, one needs six separate pieces to make a working setup:

- the reel
- the rod
- the backing
- the fly line
- the leader, or tippet
- the fly

A FLY ROD AND REEL, ASSEMBLED AND READY TO CAST

The reel is attached to the rod, and holds the backing, fly line, leader and fly, in that order. The line is fed out through the ferrules of the rod; the fly is then tied on and you are rigged up to cast. The reel, rod, backing, line and leader act in sync to present the fly to the fish in the most realistic way possible; that is, in a manner that makes the fish believe that the fly is a real insect. Ideally, the fly should resemble an easy meal that is part of its regular diet. All trout are meat eaters.

The fly fisher holds the fly rod in his or her hands, and casts into the air overhead, back and forth, creating the perfect distance and speed with which to release the fly. The fly should land where it will have the best chance of attracting a fish.

CASTING ON THE HIGHWOOD RIVER NEAR LONGVIEW, ALBERTA, CANADA

The human does not wish to be noticed by the fish, so must employ stealthy movements that create no alarms. Sudden noise or unusual splashing will make the fish wary of any object that lands upon the water. Fish are generally uncomfortable with intruders in their water.

So, in addition to walking and wading quietly, you must handle the fly rod smoothly and efficiently. Casting should be quiet, with a minimum of motion; ideally, only the rod tip and the line should be in motion.

STEALTHY STALKING ON BRONTE CREEK, NEAR BURLINGTON, ONTARIO, CANADA

Your equipment must be suited to your abilities, and to the task at hand. Scenario: You are standing at the river's edge and, through your glare-cutting polarized sunglasses, you spot some large, spotted trout swimming in a slow pool under the shade of a large tree. You want to cast to and hook one or two of these fish. If your equipment isn't properly fitted to you and your abilities, you won't be able to realize your goal. Your equipment must be easy to use, light enough to handle with skill and accuracy, and strong enough to play and subdue a fighting fish once the hook has been set.

You are a keen beginner, with basic casting technique and some fundamental knowledge. Your trusty new fly rod setup is well-matched to your needs, and you are empowered to succeed.

The Reel

A fly fishing reel has very few parts, and is quite different from a so-called spinning reel. A spindle, or hub, is mounted to an open shell. The spool that holds all the line is snapped onto the spindle and the reel is ready. A fly reel can be adjusted for either right- or left-handers.

A FLY REEL, LOADED AND READY TO GO

The rod is typically held and cast with the hand opposite the one controlling the reel so that the rod and reel both have one hand at the controls, in balance.

Instead of hundreds of feet of clear monofilament, the fly reel holds a series of specialty lines on its spool. Fly fishing line differs from common fishing line in that it is actually a super-strong nylon cord that is wrapped by a flexible polymer coat. It acts as the weighted component that carries the ultralight fly into the air and across the water.

Because the artificial fly, made mostly of fur and feathers, cannot be thrown more than a couple of feet by hand, it needs the weighted fly line to propel it forward. A spin casting rig uses the weight of the lure itself to carry it into the air and across the water.

CASTING A DRY FLY ON THE GRAND RIVER, ONTARIO, CANADA

The backing and fly line are wound onto the spool in forward turns of the reel, and pulled out by hand, or by a fighting fish, in reverse turns. The only adjustable part of a fly reel is the drag control, which is a single knob that adjusts outgoing resistance on the spool as the spool spins in reverse on the hub. The drag makes a distinctive whizzing sound, recognizable to fly fishers as a "fish on." Its main purpose is to control the rate and amount of line being fed from the reel at any moment; it directly affects the distance that a hooked fish may run while you are playing it.

THE SHELL OF THE FLY REEL, WITH SPINDLE AND DRAG MECHANISM

The reel is mostly made of steel alloys, and a good one can be purchased for less than fifty dollars at a big-box outdoor-supply store. It is the most vital moving part of your fly fishing equipment, and it must be reliable and durable. Beware of inexpensive reels, and avoid plastic altogether. One rule of thumb for fly fishing gear is that you get what you pay for. Do the research first, and get a good reel.

The Rod

A fly fishing rod is also very different from a traditional spin casting rod. First, it is generally longer because it must load and launch a long section of weighted line several yards in a straight path over the water. Flicking a steel lure 30 yards is simpler than laying out a fly line at half that distance. It requires a more-complex construction to perform a more-complex task.

A TWO PIECE, 4-WEIGHT FLY ROD IN ITS SLEEVE

Rods are built from graphite or carbon fiber, in a variety of numbered sizes, from the ultralight 3 weight to the stiff and powerful 9 weight. These numbers denote the rod's weight, strength and flex. A 5-weight rod is accepted as the best size for beginners. It is versatile and stout enough to handle large fish, while still being easy to master and rewarding to cast.

Fly rods often come in several pieces, which are ritualistically assembled at the start of the fishing adventure. There are a number of ferrules that run the length of the rod and gradually become smaller the closer to the tip they get.

The fly fishing rod is a fragile instrument, one more fragile than most fishing rods. It must flex a great deal, in a precise pattern, as the line is fed out to greater lengths on the cast. It must respond with lightness and accuracy at the instant when the hook is set. It must possess the structural strength to bend nearly in half when in use.

A FLY ROD PUT TO THE TEST ON A BIG MISSOURI RIVER
RAINBOW TROUT

Its complex structure makes a fly rod very easy to accidentally break – in car doors and at campsites, or simply underfoot at the river. The tip section of the rod, which is the end part with the greatest flex and the least strength, can easily snap, rendering the rod useless. It seldom happens during battle with an actual hooked fish.

The upside of caring for this delicate piece of equipment is in the smooth and effortless feel and power generated in casting a quality fly fishing rod. Most good fly rods are warranted for life against breakage; it is absolutely worth spending a little more money on a rod with lifetime coverage against breaks.

The reel is secured to the "seat" at the very heel or butt of the fly rod. Here it also acts as a counterweight to the casting motion. To rig up, a length of fly line is pulled out and fed by hand through the ferrules; the fly is then attached to the leader.

ATTACHING REEL TO ROD

The Backing

One-hundred yards or more of synthetic "backing" is wrapped onto the empty spool of the fly reel first off. The backing is a light, super-strong cord that ensures that you have plenty of line to feed out should a powerful fish decide to run a long distance from you before becoming tired. Since the fly line itself is fewer than 100 feet in length, the backing adds more than double that distance to the overall amount of line you have on the reel, increasing your odds of keeping even the strongest fish within reach. Backing comes on spools in assorted colors and lengths of up to 200 yards. Once it is wrapped evenly onto the spool, the fly line is knotted to the end.

REEL WITH BACKING; BASICALLY 200 FEET OF NYLON CORD

The Fly Line

The fly fishing line, as was said earlier, is actually an abrasion-resistant polymer-coated-nylon cord that slides easily through the ferrules of the fly rod for smooth casting and quick retrieval. It is around 90 feet long. A clear section of leader is attached to the end, and an artificial fly is tied onto the end of that. The weight of the line swings the fly over the water in a looping arc, which unrolls and releases first the leader and, finally, the fly.

WINDING ON THE FLY LINE

The fly line is made in an assortment of weights, colors (including clear) and lengths, and for certain uses. Lines come in floating or sinking versions, depending on where the fly is destined. Since our focus is the dry fly, we will use the floating line.

The leading ten or so yards of most floating lines are thicker and heavier than the remainder, which adds to casting power by increasing the flex of the fly rod. The extra weight loads the rod first, and carries more of the lighter line behind it. This is referred to as a weight-forward line. The floating line then rests upon the surface of the water when it lands, since it is for use with a dry fly.

Depending on the light conditions, and where the fish are lying when the fly is cast, the fly line may or may not be visible to the fish before the fly gets there. It is part of the fly fisher's art to conceal, by crafty casting and good line management, the floating line from the fish as much as possible. The neon colors of most fly lines are great for visibility when you want to see your line. When stealth is a priority, however, the clear version ensures that the fish will be less startled should your line drift over them.

Properly cared for and cleaned occasionally, a fly line will last several seasons.

THE FLOATING LINE TRAVELLING ON TOP OF THE WATER

The Leader

A fly fishing leader – the tapered length of monofilament tied onto the end of the fly line – is a well-engineered tool for the stealthy presentation of an inconspicuous fly to a wily trout. It is tapered, from stout at the rod end, where it is knotted to the fly line, to very fine and invisible at the end where the fly is tied on. It measures around nine feet long and should land straight, soft and undetected upon the water when cast, with the fly being the last object to settle on the surface. Hundreds of years ago, fly fishers spun their leaders from silk threading. Modern leaders are constructed of clear or tinted monofilament line. Leaders, or tippets, come in various lengths and strengths, depending mostly on the size of the fish you are dealing with. Beginners usually purchase their first few tapered leaders already built, eventually learning to tie their own. Factory-made leaders come in a single nine- or 10-foot strand that gradually tapers from end to end. Hand-tied leaders, however, are tied together in lengths from thick to thin. They require that the tier carries a collection of lines that differ in strength and thickness.

PREPARING TO ATTACH THE LEADER TO THE FLY LINE

Beginning at 0X (10-pound test line), the strongest and thickest, the line climbs the scale to as high as 7X (or one pound), which is thin as a spider's webbing for ultimate stealth. The thicker the tippet, the more visible it may be to the fish. Several sections of line are connected in a gradually finer succession until the last two feet of a nine-foot leader are the finest.

Selecting a leader becomes a balancing act for some fly fishers, with the question being, "Do I go for a finer tipped leader that will not alert the fish, but which may snap off the second it pulls on it? Or do I opt for the stronger and slightly thicker-tipped version, which the fish may see trailing off the fly, but which will hold onto the hook and the fish once the fight is on?" Many variables, such as water clarity, choppiness of the water and light quality, affect this choice. As your skill improves, it will become easier to play a heavier fish with a lighter-strength line in all conditions.

The basic rule with leaders or "tippets" is, the finer the line, the better your chances of hooking a fish because the line is less visible. The element of skill comes into play when the fish is fooled and the hook has been set, testing the strength of the leader at its weakest point.

TYING ON THE FLY WITH A FINE 5X LEADER

The fly rod and reel in your hand should be able to do much of the work, while you use skill and patience to let the fish tire itself under your deft control.

LETTING THE REEL AND ROD DO THE WORK IN MONTANA

Chapter 3: Flies, Flies and Tying Flies

Humans have been tossing food to fish forever. Tossing a bread crumb into a creek and watching the fish come up to eat it explains why. When someone decided to conceal a hook inside a homemade flying insect and attach it to a clear line, "fly fishing" was invented. Hundreds of years ago on the chalk streams of England, people were devising ways to fool and catch trout with tiny fake insects. They were made from all kinds of fur and feathers and wrapped onto hooks with sewing thread. The trick was to make the fly resemble what the fish were eating that day. Color, size and shape were, and still are, the main things to consider when picking out a fly to attach to your leader.

A BASIC SELECTION OF FLIES FOR FISHING THE UPPER BOW RIVER NEAR BANFF

The imitation should match the real thing. There are specific insects that fish seek out as part of their regular diet. The life of most insects has several stages and cycles. Mayflies, caddis and stone flies, which live most of their short life in or on the water, are of special interest to hungry trout. In the fishing stores you will find ready-made flies in every size, color, and species imaginable. Blue-Winged Olive, Pale-Morning Dun, Elk-Hair Caddis, Green Drake, Royal Coachman; the names are colorful and new designs emerge constantly.

Even if you failed biology, fly fishing will renew your interest in insect life. Learning enough entomology to know what is hatching and flying about in the water is priceless. The best way to start is to observe and ask questions of other fly fishers and to ask store clerks for advice on fly fishing. Be aware that most dedicated fly fishers only tell some of the truth, some of the time; it can be a culture of secrets whose quest is the perfect fly. So take most advice with a grain of salt, but remember that free advice is always worth something, especially when it comes to the complex world of insects and trout. You will learn to play the game of information over time.

A CLASSIC MAYFLY – THE BLUE-WING OLIVE

Most fly fishers eventually develop the urge to tie their own flies. It is less costly, more creative and, ultimately, more satisfying when the fish are fooled by something you created. A tabletop vise, some scissors and a thread bobbin should get you started. Thread, fur, feathers and hooks are the basic materials for most dry flies. On the market now are all-inclusive fly-tying packages that include all tools and materials, and a DVD or book of step-by-step instructions. Fly-tying is a craft that is not easily self-taught, so these kits are a great investment to get you started. They will include many of the most popular flies and patterns in use today, and will provide exposure to the much larger universe of materials and methods for tying great flies.

Of the millions of types of fur and feathers, including fur from pet dogs and feathers from canaries, most have been tried as materials in flies. Synthetic tying materials for enhancing appearance, flash, buoyancy and motion are being developed constantly. Any trip down the aisle of a well-stocked fly fishing department will open your mind to the expanding possibilities.

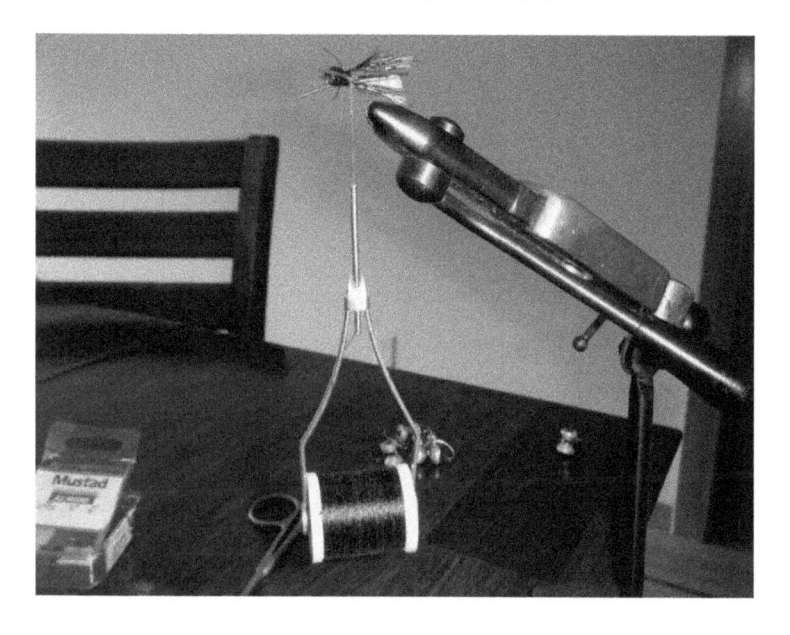

A TABLETOP TYING VISE WITH THREAD BOBBIN AND FINISHED FLY

There are special tools, including knot tiers, clamps, glue guns and magnifying glasses, for every process. The list is infinite and the art of fly-tying is a specialty in itself, with its own rewards.

Some fairly easy dry fly patterns to learn and place into your new fly box are the Elk-Hair Caddis and the Common Gnat, both of which are easy to tie and versatile to use on the water. Your first few attempts may be funny looking, but trout are fooled by silly creations all the time. Just keep tying and trying.

Chapter 4: Tools of the Fly Fisher's Trade

A TWO-SIDED FLY BOX WITH CLEAR LIDS HOLDS MANY FLIES

You now have all the parts of the fly fishing package: reel, rod, backing, line, leader and assortment of terrific flies. The last step before heading for the river is a tool kit of essential instruments you'll need. Here is a list, with descriptions:

- Clamping pliers, or haemostats (a surgical tool used to clamp blood vessels) to bend down hook barbs, to grasp hooks, and to remove hooks from the delicate mouths of fish

- Line snips (very similar to standard nail clippers) to clip line before and after tying knots
- Liquid floatant – a silicone-based fluid applied to dry flies, making them buoyant and water-repellent
- Leader straightener – a patch of leather through which the leader is drawn to straighten it and help it cast better
- Fly box – a waterproof case with a clear cover in which to arrange and store your flies for easy selection
- Landing net – a wood and nylon-mesh landing net to make life easier for you and the fish, available in all sizes
- Extra leaders – packaged, in case of tangles or a snapped line
- Vest or lanyard – to keep all your tools together and within reach; chest or fanny packs are an option as well
- Hook honer – a small sharpener to hone hook points
- Polarized sunglasses – invaluable for seeing through surface glare on the water, spotting fish and reading underwater structure
- Camera – point-and-shoot, digital waterproof model
- Life jacket – custom-made for fly fishing; small and inflatable at the pull of a cord; you may slip in the water now and then

GETTING READY TO CAST – NOTE THE NECK LANYARD
FOR HOLDING TOOLS AND LINE

This basic list will get you started. You may want to add sunscreen and bug spray. When using any chemical, remember to clean your hands before handling a fish; its body slime is a live organ and vulnerable to any contact. Other great things to have are binoculars for spying on fish-filled water without being seen; a Swiss army knife for anything and everything; a whistle should you need to get anyone's attention; matches; a flashlight; food; and water. It all depends on the adventure.

Chapter 5: Footwear and Waders

It is often necessary to wade right into the water, with the fish, in order to cast to the spot where they are holding. Bare feet are rarely an option because the bottom can be unstable or rocky. Shorts and water sandals can be great in the warm weather and waters of summer. You need to have good quality sandals with a solid tread and strong fasteners to hold you in place and to not slip off your feet; nothing is more disheartening than watching a sandal float away down the river.

GOOD QUALITY WADERS AND BOOTS ARE A JOY

There are hip and chest-high waders, both of which come in either breathable or nonbreathable materials.

Neoprene waders are made of the same material as scuba suits, and are chiefly designed to contain body heat, as well as provide absolute dryness. They are for cold weather and cold water. Neoprene in the hot weather is similar to wearing a tight-fitting garbage bag all day. For the majority of the fishing season, breathable waders made from a wide variety of layered synthetics – nylon and Gore-Tex for example – are a necessity.

Most breathable waders come with belts, storage pockets and neoprene booties sewn on at the ankle area. Better-quality models have reinforced knees, stronger stitching and tougher fabrics on the outside to resist tree branches and sharp rocks. For the very cold weather, it is still possible to wear warm layers underneath your breathable waders to keep warm, rather than opt for neoprene, which retains body heat and moisture and is hard to clean.

LAYER UP UNDER YOUR BREATHABLE WADERS TO STAY WARM ALL DAY

Once you are into some good comfortable waders, boots are next. Wading boots are designed to slide over your feet with your waders on. They are extremely stable for good support in the water, and the sole is usually made of a thick layer of felt. Felt material, when wet, will not slip on most wet surfaces, except ice. In and near the river, rocks can be covered with algae, or the mud can be very slick. Wading boots hold on remarkably well and keep you on your feet when you might otherwise be on your butt.

Some boots come with lug studs in the sole for fishing rivers with very large boulders and heavy currents; some come with rubber treads built into the sole for added traction; and still others come in combinations to suit special conditions or preferences. Felt is widely accepted as the material of choice. Felt soles can wear out after a couple of seasons, but can be easily replaced at home with a new set and some rubber cement.

A combination of good-quality wading boots and chest waders should last a long time, perhaps even a lifetime, depending on how much, where and what time of year you like to fly fish.

Chapter 6: The Waters We Fish

THE ELK RIVER NEAR FERNIE, BRITISH COLUMBIA: GREAT CUTTHROAT FISHING IN NOVEMBER

Much of the mystery and allure of fly fishing is in the waters. Water naturally seeks lower ground, finding its way through forest, mountain and prairie in falls, bends, riffles, eddies and long slow stretches. Trout live in all these places. They move around from place to place, but they have their favourite spots, referred to as "holding waters."

The first thing to consider when scouting waters is what types of fish live there. Read fishing guides and regulations for information on what is swimming where and when the seasons run. Local shops and fly fishers will have some facts worth sharing and, with a keen ear, you will hear good stories. Select your waters with care. If a certain section of the river is protected water, with perhaps a "no bait, no kill" rule in effect, it is likely a good place to fly fish because the fish will be alive and well-cared for. Fly fishers are generally conservation oriented, and often spearhead movements to protect quality fisheries.

THE HIGHWOOD RIVER IN ALBERTA, CANADA:
RUNS, RIFFLES AND POOLS

Consider food supply and cover when choosing waters. They are important elements for all fish. A steady supply of bugs and smaller fish around, combined with a shadowy hiding place, is the ideal location for a trout.

Birds such as eagles and osprey are great at catching fish. Bears and other large mammals, including humans, are also something most fish would rather avoid. Trout, therefore, make it a point to hide much of the time, and you'll rarely see one just swimming around. If, by chance, you happen to spot a few, and they sense your presence or see your shadow, watch how quickly they will scatter.

BIG WATERS SIMILAR TO THE CLEARWATER IN MONTANA HAVE A LOT OF HIDDEN STRUCTURE

The common term for holding places in moving water is "structure." The structure of a river is the most important factor in deciding where to find fish and how to cast to them. A fallen log at the bottom of a pool, a large boulder in the middle of a stream, or an overhanging branch over a deep eddy are all elements of structure. Fish instinctively seek out these safe places and will typically only move from them to chase food or other fish. The current is buffered by the structure, and it is easy for a fish to remain in one place while not using more energy than it is able to catch and consume.

Finally, water volume and current are key considerations. There must be enough current to provide sufficient dissolved oxygen, which fish need to survive. There must be enough depth to the water to supply space and cover for good numbers of fish to hold. And there must be enough constant flow, even if it is broken into channels, to carry a steady supply of food to the fish. Knowing the estimated cubic-feet-per-second (cfs) of a waterway is a great tool in gauging the fish population. Most regulated rivers are monitored for flow rate throughout the year, and they can provide a baseline for guessing the flow rates of the smaller streams you may want to check out.

THE MIGHTY BOW RIVER IN BANFF RUNS DEEP, WIDE AND COLD

Water temperature is another factor to consider once you become familiar with structure, currents and holding places. Most insects reproduce in response to ideal water temperatures.

Mayflies, a staple of any trout's diet, are triggered into mating cycles by the conditions of their environment. When the water is clear and the right temperature, the mayfly hatch is triggered. First a mayfly nymph emerges from beneath rocks in the river bed, crawls around, swims awkwardly to the surface, sheds its shell in the water, opens its wings, floats around a bit, takes off into the air and mates with other mayflies.

It is a spectacle of mass reproduction. When they are done, or spent, they literally die in midflight and spin softly back to the water, where the fish are waiting to gorge. The whole process takes less than one hour. Trout feast on the mayfly emergers, nymphs, upright flies and spent carcasses, and dedicated fly fishers match all stages of the hatch with a corresponding artificial fly, taking maximum advantage.

When picking great waters, it is wise to learn about the insects as much as about the fish living there. Other bugs such as spiders, ants and, even, bumblebees are on the trout's menu, but none are as predictable or popular as the mayfly. A water thermometer is inexpensive and a great way to gauge conditions as the season progresses, and to confirm the best temperature range for a good hatch.

Of course, the weather always plays a key role in fish activity, and air temperatures must be moderate for a good hatch to go off. If the weather is windy and very cold, it is a safe bet that the dry fly fishing will be poor in general.

While we are on bugs and hatches, another great way to read fishing water is with a bug screen, or seine. Standing in the water facing upstream, you dip the screen into the current and hold it there to collect anything and everything that may float by. It is amazing to then hold it up and see a full menu of trout food stuck in the screen. Life forms, including tiny worms and crayfish, winged insects (either dead or alive) and the tiniest of wiggling gnats, are all on display.

STANDING IN THE CENTER OF THE RIVER WILL GIVE YOU
A
GOOD READ ON ITS INSECT LIFE

Getting a good read on a potential fishing spot has much to do with the water itself, but if you look up and around at the landscape and the trees, you can round out the picture. Trout love trees because their shade and shelter provide hiding places. Trees are also home to bugs, which fall or fly from the trees into the river.

However, trees can make life miserable, and costly, for the fly fisher. When we get into casting, you will learn some ways to work around trees, but for now the best advice is to seek out more open spaces on and in the river. The main reason to give yourself some room is because of the sweeping arc of the cast. It takes a good fifty feet of room, including the space behind you, to deliver a solid cast to the water. The hook in a fly will snag easily in bushes and in the branches of trees.

LOTS OF TREES CLOSE TO THE WATER WILL LIMIT YOUR CASTING OPTIONS

Until you are tying your own flies, every time you snag or snap off a fly in a tall tree, it may cost you two dollars. This can add up at the end of the day. By selecting open places on the water, you'll reduce the number of lost flies while you are learning.

Consider the safety of the water, especially if you plan to wade in. You may come around a corner just as a large fish splashes in the middle of a deep pool. What may surprise you as you sneak into the water to cast is that the bottom drops off and the current is much stronger than you thought. You may wind up swimming downriver, and losing your rod in the process. Always know what the river bottom looks like before you decide to fish there. Polarized sunglasses help. The smooth surface hides many secrets, including depth and current features. Drownings may happen whenever people go near water, so pick your water with safety in mind, even if the biggest fish in the river is right in front of you.

BETTER TO STAY DRY ON A HUGE RIVER LIKE THE NIAGARA
(BELOW THE FALLS)

Chapter 7: The Fish

This is the last section before we get into the actual title content of the book: How to Fly fish. By now it is clear that there much to consider before you decide that you find the sport interesting, and that you are prepared to invest the time to learn and study all the elements that go into catching a fish on a fly. Now we will train our sights on the biggest challenge of all: the fish.

A FRESHWATER STEELHEAD ON THE JACKPINE RIVER NEAR THUNDER BAY

The five main species of trout that are found in North American river systems are rainbow, brown, cutthroat, brook and bull. Each has distinct markings that become easy to recognize once they are learned. Some waters hold two or three of these species together, and some waters are the exclusive habitat of a single species. Where more than one species occurs, they are known to crossbreed, creating hybrids such as the "cut-bow" or "splake."

The finest fish to engage on a fly is still considered the rainbow trout, along with its much larger migratory cousin, the Steelhead. Rainbows, pound for pound, possess the greatest acceleration and pure fighting strength of all trout. If you can get into waters known to hold rainbows, you are a lucky fly fisher. They run like crazy, leap out of the water and fight to exhaustion. They will tear off in a straight line up or downstream with more sustained power than any trout. A rainbow trout can be recognized by its stout, streamlined body shape and the brilliant pink stripe along its flank, which separates a silver lower body from a green-and-black-spotted back. Steelhead are relatives of the rainbow trout, but are distinct in that they are sea-run, migratory fish that only swim up freshwater rivers to spawn, then return to the ocean or lake for the rest of the year. Steelhead trout grow larger and more powerful than rainbows, and they were so named to reflect their unusually hard head.

A HEALTHY RAINBOW TROUT ON THE MISSOURI RIVER
ABOVE HAUSER DAM

Steelhead are fly fished with longer and stouter rods and gear. Steelhead fishing is considered the ultimate experience in freshwater fly fishing. A 15-pound steelhead, caught in the spawning seasons of spring and fall, is common on some coastal rivers. In contrast, rainbow trout, which live in freshwater all year long, will reach a mature weight of anywhere from two to eight pounds.

Brown trout are a smart and very shy species. They rest through most of the daytime hours, and feed mainly at night or in the early morning. They fight and swim with impressive power, but run out of fighting strength sooner than the rainbow trout. Their reticulated spot pattern and caramel coloring are vivid and beautiful, and provide excellent camouflage. The cutthroat and bull trout are found mostly in smaller rivers and streams close to the Rocky Mountains. They are cold-water fish, and are native to many watersheds in the West. By contrast, much of the rainbow and brown trout stock are "introduced" fish that have been placed into the waters where they live.

ANOTHER BIG FISH FROM THE MISSOURI –
THIS BROWN TROUT WAS RELEASED IN GOOD SHAPE

Cutthroat trout are quick to take a fly, and will feed all day long, even in the direct sun. A feisty and rewarding species for the beginning fly fisher, the cutthroat has a vibrant red slash beneath its jaw, which stands out from its golden colouring and tiny black spots.

Bull trout are becoming rare in many waters where once they thrived, but they can still be found in pockets throughout the Rocky Mountains. A gray, unspotted appearance distinguishes the bull trout, which can grow very large in small waters, and has the initial fighting grit of the best of the trout. Bulls are descended from the ancient char species of the cold northern rivers. For years bulls were overfished and considered easy to catch. Today, a shrinking population makes seeing a bull trout a rare treat, and it is a protected species in many cherished waterways.

A BEAUTIFUL FALL CUTTHROAT ON THE ELK RIVER,
WELL-HOOKED IN THE UPPER LIP

Brook, or speckled, trout are found all across Canada and the United States, and are by far the most interesting-looking and fun to catch of all the trout. Their markings are a masterpiece of color, pattern and vibrancy. Incredible combinations of blue and orange, gold and red are splashed across the brookie's football-like form; they are a feast for the eyes. This fish has personality, too. It is a curious and persistent chaser of flies, and will latch onto something attractive if it has to take ten runs at it. It could be a bobber, or a leaf or a piece of fluff; the brookie will swim close to inspect it at least once. Of course, the more mature fish are more cautious, but offer an equally stunning performance if hooked. If one has the luck to hook-up with the revered brook trout, even a very small one, it is a special day.

All of these fish share two character features: a small brain and a giant will. Trout have a very slow heart rate. They function on instinct and survival, like most wild species. Their eyesight is keen as a hawk's. They spot and attack prey with speed and accuracy. Their sense of smell is acute, but they often trust more in what they see than in the scent attached to it.

THIS STEELHEAD LIVES MOST OF THE YEAR IN LAKE SUPERIOR,
SPAWNING IN MAY

The trout's memory, too, is sharp and quick. Trout in heavily fished waters learn to distinguish artificial flies as intruders. Even a well-tied fly that looks exactly like a real insect may have one strand of feather out of place, which is enough to trigger the suspicion of a wily trout. Once it has decided the fly is a fake, the fish will move aside to let it pass over; eventually, it may leave the area to escape the annoyance.

Spawning cycles occur mostly in spring, affecting trout behaviour and reducing their interest in food of any kind. They are otherwise occupied for a solid month or more, and the spawn is never a productive time to fly fish. It is a great time, however, to observe large numbers of fish assembled in very shallow water, swimming and swaying and chasing one another. This spectacle usually happens in places where it is unlawful to fish, so the show is all about the adventure. The brown trout spawn in fall, and nothing compares to sitting under a crimson alder in the low light of an October afternoon, watching a dozen giant brown trout sparring and splashing about in the whitened gravel of a spawning bed.

SMALL FISH, BIG SMILE – A FEISTY BROWN TROUT ON THE
BIGHORN RIVER IN MONTANA

Chapter 8: Let's Go Fishing!

You are wearing your waders and wading boots. Your net is attached to a clip on the belt of your waders. On your head is a sensible hat and sunscreen; you sport a pair of polarized shades. On your chest are all your tools and accessories. You also have the following:

- Fly rod – the beginner's nine-foot, two-piece, 5-weight rod
- Fly reel –5-weight steel-alloy reel, with an adjustable drag
- Backing – 200 feet of yellow Dacron backing, packaged on a spool
- Fly line – yellow, 90 feet, weight-forward, floating, 5-weight
- Tapered leaders, or tippets – for now you have the manufactured kind; they are clear, nine feet long, in strength of 4X (6-pound test)
- Dry flies – a sturdy, floating plastic box of assorted flies in different sizes and color combinations, sized from 18 (small hook) to 12 (medium hook)

Assembling the parts will require your new clippers and some knowledge of a few basic knots. In order:

- Set up the reel and connect all the lines together on the spool
- Assemble the rod, and attach the reel
- Feed the line up through the ferrules of the rod until the leader is completely clear of the rod tip
- Attach the fly; it is time to start casting

Take out the reel and make sure it is set up to retrieve line the way you like it, that is by turning forward with the right or left hand (and holding the fly rod in the hand you will cast with).

Now, the backing is tied onto the spool of the fly reel and wound on by reeling in the line forward, just as you would reel in a fish. The knot used to attach the backing to the reel is basically a double slip knot, which is simple and strong.

The backing is securely on and it is time to attach the fly line to the backing. On the fly line spool will be a label that says "attach this end to backing." Because the fly line has a profile, with all the weight in the forward part, it is important that the correct end is tied to the backing. Here is the next knot, which is called a "nail knot." You can use this knot for the next two attachments.

LOOP THE LINE AND BACKING AND HOLD THEM BESIDE EACH OTHER,
FACING IN OPPOSITE DIRECTIONS

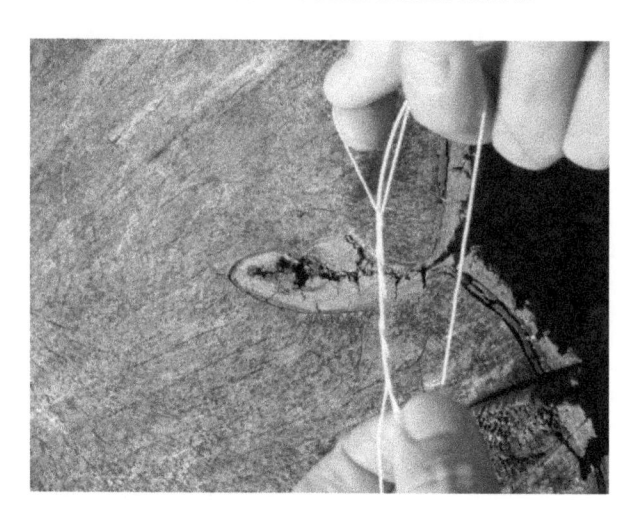

WRAP THE FREE END OF THE BACKING THROUGH THE LOOPS
AND AROUND THE FLY LINE

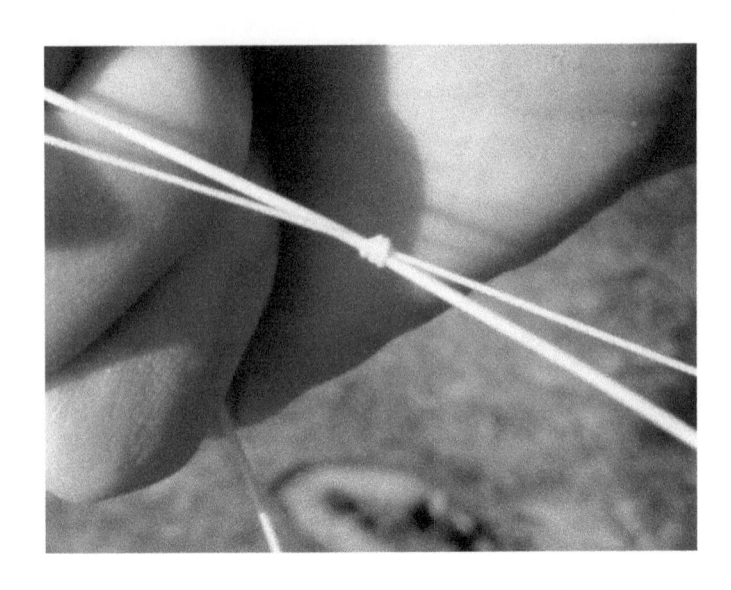

GIVE IT THREE WRAPS AND PULL IT TIGHT

CLIP OFF BOTH FREE ENDS

THE FINISHED NAIL KNOT; USE IT FOR FLY-LINE-TO-LEADER, TOO

The fly line and backing are in place, so you may attach the leader to the fly line with the exact same nail knot. The knot will become second nature with practice.

Leaders come packaged in a loosely wound loop in a small plastic envelope. When pulling the leader from the envelope, observe how the ends are wrapped inside the loop itself. Take your time unravelling the leader. The fine end, where the tippet is thinnest, will be inside the loop; the fatter end will be easier to spot and unravel. This may seem trivial, but learning how to unpack a leader is important when you're on the river and the wind is blowing and your first leader just snapped off on a tree limb while a fish is rising in front of you.

The nail knot has done its job and your reel is loaded with 200 feet of backing, 90 feet of fly line, and nine feet of tapered leader. This is the time to place the reel onto the fly rod. Reel everything in and open the sliding collar at the heel of the fly rod. The reel has tongue-like arms extending from underneath, and these fit neatly into notches in the reel seat of the fly rod. Place the reel in your preferred retrieval position, left- or right-handed, into the notches. Tighten the collar onto the reel until it is very snug. The rig is now assembled, and you may feed the line through the ferrules in the rod. The best way for nimble fingers to pass the fly line and leader up from the reel through the length of the fly rod is to

- Set your drag to an easy, but not too loose, setting
- Draw out the leader, as well as a rod's length of fly line
- Grasp the end of the fly line and feed it, one by one, through each ferrule on the rod, right through the smallest one at the tip; be sure not to miss any ferrules along the way or you'll have to do it all over again
- Once you have the tip of the fly line through the tip of the rod, pull the leader and another three feet of fly line out through the end and let it hang from the rod

It is important to note here that the end of the fly line must always be outside and beyond the tip of the fly rod when casting or playing a fish. If the leader itself is drawn back through the ferrules, it should only be when the rod is not being used, and the fly is held in the hook-keeper near the butt of the rod. Then it must be drawn completely free of the tip before casting again.

PULL THE ENTIRE LEADER, AND SOME FLY LINE, OUT OF THE ROD END BEFORE CASTING

The fly line imparts all the motion and action to the leader, and the leader slipping inside the ferrules will cause tangles. The leader may also snap more easily when rubbed against the metal edges of the ferrules. In other words, make it a habit to pull out all the leader and three feet of fly line before attaching the fly and beginning to cast. The reasons will become clearer over time.

Finally, you can select a fly from your case and attach it to the leader. We have discussed insects and fly selection to some extent, and here is where the "match the hatch" technique appears. Using your eyes, and perhaps even your seine strainer, see what, if anything, the trout are feeding on. Once you have a good sense of the insect life, you can make an educated guess as to the type, color and size of fly you should pluck from the case. If there is no activity on the water, select a "searcher" pattern similar to a moth or ant, which may attract a hungry trout.

1. With the left hand, carefully grasp the wings of the fly so as not to bend them. Hold the tip of the leader in the opposite hand and feed six to eight inches of leader through the eye of the hook from underneath the fly (with a wet fly or streamer, feed the leader down through the top of the eye; which direction it is fed from will affect how it behaves in the water). Now tie a clinch knot to attach the fly.

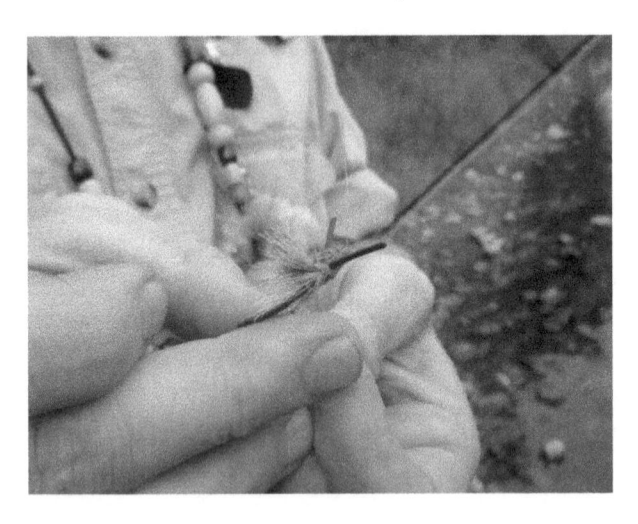

FEED THE LINE THROUGH THE UNDERSIDE OF THE HOOK WITH DRY FLIES

2. Hold the fly in the left hand and, with the right, wind the end of the leader around itself at least five times. More wraps equals more strength and a larger, more-visible knot. Keep a small open loop immediately adjacent to the hook eye. This loop is easy to keep open if you pinch it slightly. Bring the end of the leader back through the loop beside the hook eye and grasp it with the thumb and forefinger.
3. Lubricate the knot with saliva (yes, a little spit on the knot does wonders) and tighten by pulling the leader and the fly apart in opposite directions. Don't pull on the free end of the leader; just hold it in place. Give the fly a firm tug to ensure that the knot is properly tight. Use your clippers to trim off as much of the free end of the leader as possible. Fish can see the tail of a knot hanging from a fly, so the closer you can trim, the better.

**APPLY A DROP OF FLOATANT TO THE FLY TO
MAKE IT WATERPROOF AND BOUYANT**

The fly is attached and ready to cast.

Since we plan to release any fish that we catch today, the next step is to remove the barb from the hook. Hooks have tiny barbs near the tip that lodge in a fish's mouth to prevent the fish from spitting out the hook once it has been set. In the course of struggling and twisting to get free, a fish can be injured by a hook that will not dislodge. This is okay if the fish will be killed anyway, but we want this fish to go back to the river alive and healthy.

With your hemostat pliers simply bend down the barb against the hook until it can't catch on anything. The purpose of going barbless is to ease the removal of the hook from the fish once it has been caught and landed. Of course, once you remove the barb from a hook, your fish might get away before it is landed because the hook can slip out a little more easily. However, your skill and deft control of the fly rod should reduce the fish's advantage.

Once you have trimmed the knot and taken down the barb, grab your little bottle of floatant and squeeze a single drop between your fingers. Rub it gently onto the wings and body of the fly. This will keep it waterproof and floating in the water a little longer. The fluid is clear and has no scent to alert the fish. Eventually, a dry fly will get wet, so you will need to dry out the fly and reapply floatant from time to time.

Chapter 9: Casting

Experienced fly fishers make casting look easy, and it is. There are several moving parts to the process, but the main objective is tempo. Once you allow the fly rod to load and release the fly line by creating a relaxed rhythm with your hands and arms, you can concentrate on the water and the fish. What happens in the air above you directly determines what will occur on the water.

It all starts with the hands. You have decided by now which hand is your casting hand and which one is your reeling hand. Most people will cast with the right and reel, or retrieve, with the left. So the reel handle is on the left side of the rod, and is turned forward to retrieve. By the way, a fly reel is never manually turned in a backward direction; it spins backward only when line is being stripped out, either by hand or by the actions of a fish that has been hooked.

The casting hand has one function: to grasp the cork handle and perform all the tasks, such as casting or playing a hooked fish, of wielding the fly rod itself.

The retrieving hand, on the other hand, performs two specific duties, both involving line control.

The retrieving hand operates the reel, turning the handle to bring in line. It also controls the section of line called slack, which is four to six feet of fly line that is stripped off the reel and held loosely in the retrieving hand to offer more precise control of all the movements in the casting and drifting of the fly.

Each hand is always at work. The retrieving hand switches between slack line and reel control, depending on what is being done: casting, drifting, mending or reeling in the fly line. The slack line is held firmly to counter the force of casting, and then released with the actual cast. More line is stripped off the reel once the fly is cast, and is held tight against the light force of the drifting fly. In other words, the slack line should not actually go slack, but be held in the fingers of the retrieving hand to offer a manual counterforce.

EACH HAND DOING ITS JOB ON THE CAST

Find an open area, not necessarily near any water, to get familiar with the mechanics of the fly cast. You want to get to know your equipment and how it will work for, and with you. An actual fly with a hook can be substituted for a fluffy piece of yarn, which won't catch on anything around or on you. Simply tie a double knot around a one-inch length of bright yarn.

Now, with your casting hand, grasp the fly rod with a thumb-up grip, cradling the handle comfortably in your fingers. Feel the weight of the rod as it tips forward. Flex the rod in a light whipping motion, back and forth, to feel how it reacts to the slightest hand and finger action. Notice how the thumb applies all the forward force, and the fingers draw the rod backward. This is the correct grip for all casting.

Loosen the drag setting on the reel until you can easily draw out the entire leader and several feet of fly line. This slack line can lie on the ground at your feet; it will soon be picked up and cast into the air by the fly rod.

With the index finger of your casting hand, pinch the fly line against the handle of the rod so that it will not feed out as you cast the first length of line into the air.

With your reeling hand, loosely hold the slack line in your fingers as you prepare to cast. You must always have both hands engaged in casting and retrieving line, which is referred to as "line management."

At this point, you are poised to cast some line out, and your hands are relaxed in front of you, with one holding the fly rod and one holding the slack line. You may now gently snap the rod upward and back, causing the fly line to lift and travel back behind your head. Once it has unfurled behind you, gently push the rod forward with your thumb, in a light snapping motion, and the line will come back over you, travelling forward. As it unrolls and flattens, set up to snap it backward again. This is the basic motion of casting a fly.

**THE LOOP, LINE BEING PROPELLED FORWARD;
NOTE THE RELAXED GRIP ON THE FLY LINE**

It is important to lift your elbow and keep the rod tip high in the air as you begin to cast line. The wrist should be firm and the grip should be comfortable but secure. The fly rod will flex a great deal as the line is drawn in both directions, and it takes very little arm and wrist energy to flex the rod and move the line back and forth.

Keep the fly line travelling high above you, and watch how the loops form in both directions. When the loop flattens, the rod is referred to as loaded, which means the maximum force of line weight and momentum has been reached – and you can the line back the other way or counter-cast. Back and forth, back and forth; there is a definite rhythm to fly-casting. Rushing the back or forward cast will disrupt this rhythm, which can lead to complications, such as tangles or snags.

The fly, leader and line must not touch the ground behind or in front of you. It should stay aloft as you cast back and forth in an easy rhythm, with your elbow high and cocked, and your wrist flicking in tempo. The rod will do all the work if you allow it to.

Some teachers use musical methods to illustrate the ideal tempo of a fly cast. Tick, tock, tick goes the metronome. The fly caster keeps time with the snap of the rod overhead. The hands of a clock are used to describe the range of travel; the front and back casts should remain within the hours of ten and two o'clock.

Dropping the rod tip lower than ten and two will allow the line to travel downward, which causes a whipping action on the counter-cast, which leads to snapped-off flies and tangles. As you improve, you should not need to flick the rod any farther than eleven o'clock and one o'clock. But you will develop your own style eventually, at which point the rules become yours.

Breathing is important. It relaxes and enhances tempo in any sport, so try to inhale on the back cast, and exhale on the front cast.

LINE FLATTENING OUT ON THE BACK CAST – ELBOW UP, WRIST UP

You now have the fly line making nice arcs above your head, back and forth, without any whipping or snapping sound – just fluid, relaxed movement of your arm and wrist. This sweeping of the line back and forth to establish tempo and momentum is referred to as "false casting."

At this point, you may release and feed out the rest of the line at your feet. Unpinch your index finger on the back cast, and allow the line to travel up and out of the rod and into the air. Things get more difficult as the amount of line in the air increases. Slightly more force and a slower tempo are needed to keep more line up there, but not more motion, just more crisp flicks of the wrist and a nice high elbow acting as the anchor.

Timing changes slightly as well. As more line is added, the tempo must slow ever so slightly to allow the extra line to unfurl and fully load the rod, before applying the counter-cast. Keep breathing, and watch the line as it travels.

HOMING IN ON THE TARGET, READY TO RELEASE THE FLY

Now you may consider actually picking a target point, either on the water or in the driveway, to land your fly. You may need more line to cover the distance to the target so, at this point, between the front cast and the back cast, you may, with your reeling hand, actually "strip" more line off the reel and release it into the air on the back cast. This is a complex action but no more difficult than achieving good tempo.

The stripping motion is done with a reverse grip of the thumb and forefinger on the fly line where it exits the reel. As your line unfurls on the front cast, unpinch the line under your index finger. Now you are controlling the fly line with your retrieving hand. Grasp the fly line as you continue false casting and hold it comfortably. With the line in front of you, peel off an arm's length of line from the reel and release it with the momentum of the back cast.

Let the line travel up and out of the rod and into the air until you feel you have enough line to reach your target. Then peel out one more length of line and, on the next front cast, release everything forward. The line should unfurl in a smooth line straight ahead, the leader should follow and, finally, the fly should reach the end of its flight and settle onto the water's surface. You have just cast a fly upon the water.

There are two key elements to keep in mind when casting a dry fly. If you are right-handed, the best side of the river to fish from as you look downstream is the right side, and vice versa if you are casting left-handed. This is because dry flies should always be cast upstream from where you are standing. Fishing a dry fly demands what is referred to as a "drag-free drift." In other words, the fly should float freely and naturally down the current, into the trout's line of sight, without line or leader affecting its travel.

MENDING LINE TO CREATE A DRAG FREE FLOAT –
FLY DRIFTING AHEAD OF THE FLY LINE

Drag occurs when the fly and the line are drifting downstream at different rates and the line pulls at the fly. Casting the line upstream offers the fly fisher a drag-free drift, since the fly line is at an angle in the water, facing upstream, where it has the least amount of water force acting upon it.

As the angle of the line becomes perpendicular to the current, the force pushing the line downstream increases and the line begins to form a downstream arc, which eventually pulls the fly along with it, effectively ending the cast as the fly is submerged and dragged through the water.

So, to review, you are standing in or near the water, with your casting hand on the downstream side, and you are aiming your cast upstream to achieve the best float. The last thing to consider is where you are positioned in relation to your target fish. Trout swim upstream, directly into the current, most of the time.

CAST UPSTREAM OF THE FISH,
SO THE FLY FLOATS NATURALLY BACK INTO VIEW

A feeding fish will generally hold a position facing upstream, watching for food to come by. Because it is swimming forward and looking ahead, the best place for you to stand is behind the fish, where it can't see you. So, try to position yourself below the fish and then cast upstream, above the fish, with the object being a drag-free float into the spot you've picked out.

As you cast and release the fly forward, it is important to give the fly rod a good flick in the direction of the landing target, and keep the rod tip high. The tendency will be to dip the rod as you make the cast, which will cause you to lose accuracy and power. You want to flex and stop the rod tip with a firm wrist flick and let all the line run out until the fly is just hanging there in space for an instant, before fluttering gently to the water. Grip the rod using your thumb to push forward, and your fingers to stop it suddenly. It will come with practice. This combination of patient tempo, well-controlled line momentum and length, and crisp delivery of a fly that ends its journey with a soft landing on the water is the ideal presentation.

THIS BIG BROWN LIKED THE PRESENTATION AND GULPED THE FLY TRUSTINGLY

The artificial fly should resemble a real insect in appearance, but selling the package to a wily trout depends a lot on how it is delivered. In other words, presentation is everything, and it is the delicate art of mastering good presentation that consumes fly fishers for a lifetime.

Nothing compares to spying for half an hour on a feeding trout; observing its rhythm and ease of swimming; noticing exactly which bugs it selects from the surface; gathering yourself and your skills; getting into position; and gently dropping the right fly with a solid presentation directly in its feeding zone.

As the trout faithfully rises and takes the fly, you may get a shot of adrenalin. It takes a lot of preparation and practice to reach that moment. In addition, there is usually only one chance to fool a trout with an artificial fly, so it is important to keep calm and set the hook well in order to continue the adventure.

GOOD CONCENTRATION MAKES GOOD PRESENTATION

If you have the supreme satisfaction of seeing the fish rise and take the fly, you can lift the rod and set the hook with good timing. However, these moments can be rare, so you must learn to react to other cues indicating that a fish has taken hold of the imitation. Your visibility may be obscured by water or objects around you, so be alert for a splashy sound as the fish attacks the bug or for a sudden pull on the line as it turns away. A fly rod is a very sensitive instrument, and any twitch in the line will be transmitted to your hand, so you should be able to set the hook with a mere flick upward.

Once the fly is on the water and into its drift, the line must again be pinched against the handle with the index finger of your casting hand. This sets the line length and readies you for a hook set. Keep any slack line in your retrieving hand. Keep the rod tip pointed at the fly, following it as it travels down the stream.

How the fly line and leader behave in the water will determine how the fly will appear to the fish. If the fly is flipping sideways or dragging unnaturally in the current, the fish will be confused and may avoid the bug altogether, so managing your line on the water is just as important as when it is airborne.

"Mending" line refers to flipping the line that is on the water either upstream or downstream, depending on what you want to achieve. With the dry fly, mends are usually made upstream. The purpose of mending is to both improve the quality of the fly's drift on the water and to extend the length of the fly's drift.

By mending, or flipping, the line back upstream as the fly travels down, you delay a swinging movement of the line that will cause the fly to skitter in an arc downstream as it follows along. The object of a good cast followed by a steady drift is, once again, to make the fly move in a convincing way that will attract a fish toward it.

To mend line, wait until the fly has been cast and landed upstream. Now, observe its path as it drifts downstream. The fly line, with more mass and more water moving against it, may drift ahead of the tiny fly and cause it to speed up, pulling it downstream and across the water. To correct this, drop the tip of the rod almost to water level, draw in as much slack line as possible without affecting the fly's movement, and crisply flick the rod tip upward and to the left (or upstream). Ideally, you will flip a length of fly line out of the water and back to where it is even with the fly in the current; this takes practice.

A ROLL CAST: NOTE THE LINE COMING UP OFF THE WATER AND ROLLING FORWARD

There are two other important techniques you should add to the basic casting motion, both of which improve distance control. One will extend your range for hard-to-reach spots, and the other will help you cast in very tight spots where there is not much room to cast behind you.

The first is the "double haul." Basically, this refers to stripping line off the reel in sync with the back cast, releasing it on the front cast, and then doing it as many times as necessary before actually casting the fly onto the water. It is an action that quickly adds to the length of fly line travelling in the air, and increases your reach.

The double haul demands good line speed and a crisp casting motion because the weight and force increase with each arm's length of line you add on the back cast. It is both hands working at once, creating force with the stripping hand and transferring it to the casting hand, then releasing the fly at the target. It is actually easier to execute than it is to explain, and you will use it often.

RELEASING AFTER A DOUBLE HAUL – EXTRA POWER AND DISTANCE

The other great tool to master is the roll cast, a simple forward flicking action that helps you work around close spaces. The roll cast isolates the casting action into a forward snap without a back cast. It is used when there is no room to back cast or generate line speed the traditional way. Instead, with the line lying slack in the water, the rod tip is lifted slowly and then flicked sharply forward, causing the fly line to follow in a loop and lay out toward the target.

The roll cast is invaluable on smaller streams with close tree cover and bushy banks. Simply lift and "roll" the line forward with a flick of the rod tip; it is another technique you are sure to master and use frequently as conditions change.

At this point you, have cast and landed the fly. It is drifting; you are mending and keeping it on a straight float. It looks just like the rest of the real bugs that are floating in the current. As it approaches the place you've aimed for, your body naturally goes very still and your focus becomes intense. Suddenly, the snout of a fish breaks the water and engulfs your fly. What now?

USING THE ROD'S STRENGTH TO HOLD A
FISH FROM ESCAPING, TO NO AVAIL

Chapter 10: Hooking Up and Playing

Lift the elbow and flick the wrist upward while, at the same moment, you pull downward with the slack line in your retrieving hand. These are two simple hand motions that must be in sync. The rod tip applies most of the force and direction to the setting of the hook, and the retrieving hand provides the instant tension that draws the hook back toward you. This is the moment when the fly should become hooked in the lip of the fish.

Sometimes the fish attacks but misses the fly. You lift the rod and the fly sails over your head, landing somewhere behind you. Simply pick it out of the bushes and gather yourself for another try in a few minutes. Time will tell if the fish really wanted that fly, and you may get a second chance.

If the hook is set, you will know it. For lack of a better term, all trout "freak out" when they are first hooked. Hooks sting, and suddenly the fish's movement is being restrained by a foreign object in its mouth. It will wriggle and fight once it is aware of its predicament. You must focus on keeping the rod tip high, and pinching the line under your finger. Maintain your two-fingered grasp on the fly line with your retrieving hand.

The fish will want to escape, and quickly. You may need to release your grip on the fly line, letting the fish take line and go where it wants. Keep the tip of the rod pointed upward as the fish runs. The reel will now take over as you release the line and the fish tightens up the slack. The fish is now "on the reel," which is exactly where you want it to be. This means that there is no longer any slack for you to manage with your retrieving hand because it is all in the water with the retreating fish.

LETTING A RAINBOW RUN ON THE REEL

The light drag setting on your reel will allow the fish to run with some more line from the reel, resulting in a "whizzing" sound as the spool spins in reverse on the hub. You can adjust the drag here if it is too firm or too loose. You don't want the spool to overspin and tangle up line. Let the fish take a long run this time. Move your retrieving hand toward the reel, but wait until the fish slows down before beginning to reel in.

The line will go slack as the fish runs out of steam. At this point you must begin to reel in the fish by keeping a constant tension on the line. Play it by ear, and by feel. Too much force may cause the hook to come free or the leader to snap. The next move in the game is up to the fish: run again, change direction, head downstream, or simply hunker down under a log.

One trout tactic you must react to in a special way is the leaping fish. A fish will jump out of the water in a panicked attempt to shake the hook out of its mouth, and it will often succeed. But you can be prepared to counter this move by "bowing to the king."

A hooked fish often heads for deeper water to get away, then suddenly turns and charges at the surface, breaking the water and twisting about in the air. This changes the dynamics of the rod and line action.

It is relatively easy to keep a constant tension on the fish while it is swimming underwater; the fly line is submerged and the water is acting on everything evenly. When a fish takes to the air, however, the line lifts out of the water with it, creating enough slack to give the fish a brief advantage. A high rod tip and a firm wrist at this point will cause you to pull at the free slack and, with no water to equalize the line tension, the line will instantly pull tight between you and the airborne fish.

This can result in a snapped line or a spit-out fly, and a vanished trout. The best counter-move to a leaping fish is to instantly lower the rod tip so it is pointing directly at the fish. This will release the tension and allow the slack to remain constant, helping you to avoid the sudden yank that may set the trout free. It feels unnatural, and you must fight the urge to keep pulling on the fish, rather than paying out some slack, but doing so only lasts for a short time. Basically, just loosen your grip for a moment. Once the fish has landed back in the water, bring up the rod tip and apply tension as before.

Even a strong rainbow trout, the fastest fish and hardest fighter of all, will tire quickly under the stress and exertion of this ordeal. As you draw it back slowly toward you, patiently reeling in only the amount of line it gives you, the fish may appear spent of energy and ready to bring to hand. However, when it gets close enough to see you and the net looming overhead, a trout may show a sudden burst of panicked energy and take off for another run.

KEEP THE ROD TIP HIGH AS YOU PLAY A FEISTY FISH

For this reason, once again, the rod tip must remain vertical, and the drag should remain open enough to let the fish go for another tear. Its tactic may change at any time, and as long as it runs upstream or across the current, you have a slight advantage. Even if you have to take a few steps downstream to improve the angle of play, the current will carry the fish back toward you.

However, the trout has another weapon in its arsenal, and this is the downstream run. If the fish turns downstream, and there is enough water moving that way, things can get challenging for the fly fisher, and a counter-move is in short order. If you have seen the film *A River Runs Through It,* a must-see for fly fishers of all levels, you will recall the character played by Brad Pitt hooking a trout in a strong current. The fish instantly heads downstream, at which point Pitt must follow, floating and flailing down the river until he is able to subdue the fish.

The realistic part of this scene is in the sudden advantage a fish gains when it swims with the current in order to escape. The force of a two or three pound trout propelling itself against the fly line is multiplied several times by the added force of the flowing water, and the extra power can be felt immediately. The fly line, too, is being carried down the river, and this surge of resistance will pull the rod tip down and strain the leader. Here you may consider whether all the knots you've tied will be enough to hold the fish, or whether you will move downstream with the fish in order to reduce the pull being exerted on the fly knot especially.

If you stay put, on or near the shore, you risk losing the fish and your fly as the force of its retreat increases with the amount of line it takes. There is even the chance that you may be "spooled," which means that the fish runs away not only with your fly but with your fly line, which can snap off at the backing knot under enough accumulated strain. Getting spooled is a quick way to end the fishing day.

It should be mentioned that it takes a strong and fair-sized trout to create many of these scenarios. Most of the fish in a certain river or stream may not have the power to spool you or snap off a fly in the air, but your technique will decide every battle, and you will eventually find and hook some large trout in your adventures.

A BIG FISH! TIME TO GET INTO THE WATER

When a fish turns downstream, the first thing you should consider is the terrain you may have to walk or wade through to follow the fish as it moves. Going swimming should be a last resort. Stay on shore if possible; working through the weeds and bushes on dry land is much safer than stumbling along a river bottom that may hide logs, rocks or pools.

Obviously you need enough room and clearance to keep the rod tip flexed and the fly line free of shoreline snags. When you are closer to the fish, you can enter the water again to close in on the fish and end the battle.

This brings up the next stage, which is closing the distance and finishing the job. The fish has run three or four times. You have patiently played it as it jumped and turned downstream and generally challenged your skill. As the line and rod relax somewhat, you can feel that the fish is growing weary. The runs become shorter, and it gets easier to reel in more line. You may now get your first real look at the fish up close as it swims in the shallows nearby.

This is a great moment. You are able to identify the species and get a good sense of its size and markings. Now is the time to tighten down the drag control, still keeping the rod high in the air. With the drag set a little tighter, you will be able to keep tension in the line while going about the task of landing the fish.

Bringing the fish in will require taking your hand from the reel and grabbing your landing net. Keep a firm pinch on the fly line with your rod hand. Bear in mind that a tighter drag setting allows for no sudden bursts of power by the fish, so be sure that it is truly out of gas before tightening down the drag and starting to bring the fish to hand.

NETTING THIS FISH ELIMINATED THE STRESS ON EVERYONE

As the fish grows tired, the balance of power shifts and you, the fly fisher, can dictate the next chain of events. With its last few surges of will it may attempt to dart away from you with a flip of its powerful tail. Now you may actually steer the fish's movements with the tip of the rod.

From the vertical position, you can tilt the rod to the left or right of you, maintaining tension and changing the angle of retrieval. This will move the head of the fish and confuse its sense of direction, adding to its mounting fatigue.

The moment of truth is evident when the fish actually rolls toward its side rather than swimming upright. This is the time to bring it close to your feet and make contact. With the drag set tight and the rod held high above you, patiently draw the floundering fish toward you.

Reel in all of your line, but make sure to keep the leader outside of the rod tip. This should give you about nine feet of leader to work with; it should match the length of the fly rod and draw the fish closer.

The reason for keeping the tippet from sliding through the ferrules and into the rod has to do with the knot holding the tippet and fly line together. Even the best tied and trimmed nail knot cannot change the fact that the two lines are of different thicknesses, and the knot itself is large enough to snag on the last ferrule at the tip of the rod should the fish suddenly start to struggle and need more line. Keeping the end of the fly line outside the tip of the rod prevents any snagging at the moment of truth, which can be awkward enough.

Chapter 11 – Landing and Releasing the Fish

An exhausted fish now puts its life in your hands. The next few minutes are important ones. How the fish is handled, either by hand or by net, determines its odds for survival. A net makes it easy to evenly sling and hold the fish under its entire body length, reducing stress on its backbone. More important, the net allows for a hands-free capture. Getting hold of a slippery fish is a challenge, especially while it thrashes about in the water. Human hands are not suited to catching fish; the grabbing and squeezing is hard on fragile organs and on the protective slime covering its body.

Some fly fishers take pride in their ability to cradle or tail a caught fish by hand, but the fish suffers from the contact. Always bring your net to the river. It's possible that you may even help land the biggest fish of the day, hooked by someone who forgot her net. There are a few gadgets, such as a spring clip or extendable shock cord (which you may attach to your vest or waders), available to keep your landing net within reach and out of your way.

By far the slickest method yet is the two-piece magnetic clip, which can be hooked anywhere on your gear and uses simple magnets to hold the net to the clipping device. When it's time to grab the net, the magnets simply pull apart.

Once your fish is calm enough to be caught, it is great to have a friend holding the net as you steer the fish toward it; it allows you to work the rod and reel with two hands. If you are working solo, hold the net underwater, facing the fish, and lead the fish's head first toward the opening with a high rod tip. A brisk sweep of the net under the fish, and a light lift should be all it takes to finish the job.

THIS STEELHEAD WAS WORTHY OF A PICTURE, THEN A GENTLE RELEASE

It is not always necessary to raise the fish entirely out of the water, though this is a time when others may want to see your catch or get a photo. Take a breath, and keep as much of the fish in the water as possible. A resting trout can recover quickly and a wooden net frame floats nicely around the fish as you regroup. Consider now what you will do with the fly rod in your hand as you go about the next step, removing the hook.

Placing the rod on the ground is a thought, especially in the excited moment. However, if you are standing in the water or some thick bushes, simply tuck the reel under your armpit with the rod tip pointing up and away from any snags. Now you have two hands to remove the hook, and you still have the rod.

If the hook is in the upper lip, the ideal spot, pliers won't be necessary. Simply grab and twist; the barbless hook will pop free. If the fish has engorged the hook deeper, or even swallowed it, you will need to gently cradle it near the head, reach in and grasp the hook shaft with your pliers. You may need to twist or push the hook slightly deeper to free it. Time is of the essence because this is easily the most stressful operation on the fish.

Hook removal takes a deft touch, which is learned over time and trial. For now, your hands may shake a bit but it will soon be over and the trout will swim away. Once you have the hook free, be sure not to drop it into the mesh of the net. It will snag there and make more work for you.

A QUICK LIFT FOR THE CAMERA AND THIS RAINBOW IS BACK IN THE RIVER

With any luck, you will have the camera within reach or someone is already aiming as you work. Getting your smiling face in the picture is crucial, so lifting the fish with two hands is okay; just don't squeeze. Before the trout is released back to the river, it should be able to hold itself upright and not roll sideways. You want this fish to be feisty and ready to go when you send it back home. To feed it some oxygen, you can point its head into the flowing current. This will push some water through its gills and revive it quicker. When its body starts to undulate in the water, it is doing fine and you can direct it bodily toward freedom. Make sure the net, line and hook are out of its path. A splashy flip of the tail should be the last you see of this fish but do watch until it goes out of sight.

You may now cheer and high-five whoever is near, even the dog. There are a few things to consider as you reflect: The fly you selected was a good choice; the water you selected contains fish that are feeding and responsive to the fly; your knots held, meaning they were properly tied with the right selection of tippet strength; and, finally, there are probably more fish in or near the same location so you should take another cast or two before moving elsewhere.

Chapter 12: When to Fly fish

The best time to fish is whenever you have the chance. Free time is a luxury, and fly fishing is a privilege. Unique to fly fishing is the fact that poor weather can be the best time to be out there. Fish don't mind the rain; low-pressure systems often trigger hatches, especially in the spring and fall when the Blue Wing Olives are active. As long as you can keep your hands warm for tying knots and such, rain can be a minor distraction. Dressing for the elements will negate any discomfort and keep your attitude positive. To complement your waders, a breathable waterproof jacket is a must, especially if you live in cold or mountainous regions where the seasons are brief and the weather changes quickly. Sealed cuffs, a high zip-up collar and a full hood are great features to look for. A great jacket will become your best friend on the river.

Another benefit of fly fishing in foul weather is the absence of competition for good spots. You rarely see anyone out there when it is bad, so you may find that you have the river to yourself.

Fine weather, with lots of sunshine and warm temperatures, typically has a negative effect on dry fly fishing through the midday. All trout are wary of being seen, especially by the predatory raptors such as eagles and osprey, which are both superb fishers. Bright sunshine illuminates clear water and often sends fish into the depths to cower. Water temperatures rise in the midday and tend to slow down feeding as well.

There are exceptions, such as coldwater cutthroat and brook trout streams with not much water and fewer food sources where the fish feed fearlessly all day. These spots are jewels, mostly found on the eastern slopes of the Rockies and in streams across the Northern Hemisphere.

BENEATH THE HAUSER DAM ON THE MISSOURI; THE DAM ONCE BROKE, LEAVING DEBRIS EVERYWHERE

Another exception to the hot-and-sunny rule is to be found in the lower elevations of the Rockies and foothills, where the rivers, such as the mighty Bow, have tall grassy banks. Here you can experience the awesome energy of fishing with grasshopper flies. Mostly constructed of layered multicolor foam and floppy rubber legs, the grasshopper is the ultimate summertime fly in the west.

One benefit is it need not be fished extremely well to get results. In the scorching days of July and August, when the buzz of cicadas is constant, grasshoppers abound in the prairie grasses and often end up floating in the rivers. They tend to struggle in the water, and make a big, easy meal for a hungry trout. These fish learn from an early age to take notice when hoppers are on the water. Their response is immediate and impressive.

Bright sunshine or not, the rewards of snapping a hopper from the surface outweigh the risks, especially for the larger, more aggressive fish. A grasshopper-fly cast to the right fish on a sunny day will trigger an attack unlike any other. It is a large, clunky fly to cast but the weight helps it fly farther. A hopper fly may not always land upright, but this clumsiness mimics the real insect and the fish are seldom put off by sloppy casting.

In short, hopper fishing is fun in the sun, though, generally, a hot summer day is best for napping in the shade by the river. The fish don't shut down completely but they tend to ignore surface activity, aside from that from hoppers, much of the year.

The best option at this time of day is to switch over to nymph or streamer fishing, which calls for different lines, flies and casting techniques not covered here. These are considered very productive methods for catching trout all year, and they offer their own challenges and rewards. Basically, you are putting the fly down into the fish rather than luring it to the surface. A well-equipped fly fisher has more options and a longer season with setups for nymph and streamer fishing.

At sunset, the dry-fly action starts up again. The shifting conditions of the dusk hours can trigger large mayfly hatches, while simultaneously drawing fish out of their hiding places. Changes in light and temperature will attract rising fish to a previously quiet stretch of river, and the evening hours mark the start of the day for many fly fishers. They will cast until pitch darkness makes it impossible to see the fly. The sounds of fish slapping the water may follow them as they reluctantly pack up to leave.

Often you will spend a long, fine day fly fishing and see nothing, convinced that there is not a fish within a hundred miles. But if you are lucky enough to stick around for the sunset, your opinion may change. A snout will break the surface in a hole you fished for two hours. Shallow stretches of the river near the shore may suddenly boil quietly with the arrival of hungry trout. An evening hatch is a true spectacle, as is the feeding frenzy that follows.

THE HIGHWOOD IS ENCLOSED BY TREES AND CANYON, GREAT FOR A MAYFLY HATCH

The mayflies start to rise en masse as if a switch had been turned on. As they dance and hover silently above the river and the trees, your attention is suddenly captured by a slurping sound and a swish of water. The trout react in different ways to a hatch, sometimes shunning the menu and waiting for a different insect of choice. But in the glory days of summer, it is a good bet that a hatch at dusk will draw most of the fish to the surface.

Many streams and rivers in the West flow through some type of sunken land structure, such as a canyon or narrow valley. These are remnants of a torrential glacial runoff millions of years ago. To be on a river between rising walls during an evening hatch is amazing. The insects swarm in the enclosed ravine and the sound of feeding fish echoes softly across the water. Voices can be heard calling out "fish on!" accompanied by the whiz of a fly reel spinning out line.

The same is true of the early morning hours before sunrise. Trout will often still be on the overnight feed, and the warmth of daylight will trigger hatches at dawn much as they do at dusk. Things tend to slow down as the sun moves overhead, but the morning mayfly hatch can also be a very productive time.

In the spring and fall, the dry-fly game changes. Water temperatures are generally colder in the shoulder seasons, slowing the metabolism of a trout, which means its appetite tends to drop off. Fish are less inclined to move very far to find food, even if it floats directly over their snouts. With the shortened days, the appearance of the sun can have a motivating effect on sluggish fish, warming up the water and triggering insect and fish activity for a brief window of time.

But spring, fall and winter months bring more unstable and diminished fly fishing conditions, which does not mean that the season is over. It just means the dry-fly season is closing down, and it is time to learn about nymph and streamer fishing, or book a trip to New Zealand where the summer is just beginning.

To sum up, when the weather is fine, dry fly fishing peaks at both dusk and dawn. When the weather is off, the fishing can be great. Something to bear in mind with foul weather is that fish don't like when the barometer is moving, especially downward. Incoming low-pressure systems often send the fish into hiding, but once things stabilize, they reappear.

A similar principle applies to the cycles of the moon, which are said to directly influence the quality of fishing. Calendars that use lunar cycles to predict when the best fishing days will occur can be found at the local gas station, and many consider the science to be sound. Full moons are generally poor times to fish, while the weeks before and after the full moon are often the best.

Chapter 13: Where to Fly fish

We've already discussed selecting waters for structure, surroundings and layout, but not specifically where to find these things. The absolute best advice this book can offer on where to fly fish is based on firsthand experiences in the spectacular trout waters of Southern Alberta and British Columbia, and the great state of Montana. This is the eastern slope watershed of the Rocky Mountains, and is home to countless blue-ribbon trout fisheries of every size and character.

The major cities serving this huge area include Calgary, Cranbrook and Billings, all of which have major airports. Rivers throughout this triangle have several things in common, all of which combine to make it a fly fisher's ultimate experience, especially when it comes to dry fly fishing.

THE ELK RIVER, IN FERNIE, BRITISH COLUMBIA, IN NOVEMBER

The water is cold, most of the time ranging from 50 degrees Fahrenheit to 60 degrees Fahrenheit, which is ideal to support a trout population. Trout need cold water year round to thrive and survive, which is why the warmer waters of the Midwest hold mainly bass and pike species, warmwater fish that have a less sophisticated diet and more resilient metabolism.

The fish are well-fed. Mayflies are abundant, with several species ranging throughout the region and providing a year-round food source. Lots of other insects, such as the giant stonefly and various water-beetle species, contribute to the trout's diet, and the river bottom is home to crayfish, leeches and worms of all kinds. The terrestrial diet, including grasshoppers, spiders and ants, also helps to keep the fish healthy.

The fishing season is long. Quality dry fly fishing starts up in May on the Bow near Calgary, Canada, and continues well into late October on the Elk in Fernie, British Columbia, only 300 miles to the southwest. The Missouri River in Montana also heats up in early May and offers amazing dry fly fishing into November. It should be noted that all the rivers and streams in the western region are subject to regular spring runoff, which can be massive, extending through the entire month of June and into July. The rivers become high, muddy and dangerous, completely impossible to fish or wade. It is hard to conceive of a population of trout surviving such a sustained deluge of silt and debris, but they manage quite well.

The fly fishing society is large and well-established. Shops, guides, generous landowners, conservationists, and friendly, respectful fly fishers make up a dynamic culture in the West. Information and instruction are readily available, and the more people you meet, the more tips you get on hot spots to fish, and the right flies to use. There is a tangible sense of the history of fly fishing, as well as of the connection of people to special places.

There is amazing fly fishing all over the globe. As your skills and knowledge increase, you may be drawn to Belize to sight-cast to the powerful bonefish; to Northern British Columbia to wield 13-foot "spey" casting rods for 20-pound Pacific steelhead; to the wilderness of Newfoundland to cast flies at giant Atlantic salmon; or even to northern Ontario to cast three-inch streamers with steel leaders to giant northern pike or muskie. The list goes on, and it would take several lifetimes to fly fish all the great waters of the world, not including those that have not been discovered yet.

Where and when you fly fish depends on your budget of both time and money. Getting started close to home is the best way to learn. North America for the most part is a giant wet land mass that was once the bottom of a great ocean. No matter where you live on this continent, chances are you are close to some type of moving water. Your new hobby will require that you study maps and find the water; do research and find the fish; and have your gear ready to go when the opportunity arises.

Chapter 14: Guides and Drift Boats

Dollar for dollar, there is no more worthwhile investment for a beginning fly fisher than to hire a guide for a day on the river. Not only will you probably hook into some actual fish, you'll gain a priceless education in a very short time. The opportunity to be guided to a quality stretch of trout water, and shown how to fish it by an expert, cannot be matched in a hundred days spent trying to figure it out for yourself. Lessons such as fly selection, insect life, casting into crosscurrents, even spotting fish where you never would have looked, are all chunks of data that will make up the wealth of knowledge you will absorb by day's end.

MACKENZIE DRIFT BOATS ON THE BIGHORN IN MONTANA
A BUSY RIVER WITH BIG TROUT

One of the best features of guided fishing is that you do not need to own any gear to try it out. Most guides are affiliated with fly shops, which supply all the equipment for your day, including rods, reels, leaders, flies, waders and boots. A guided adventure is an affordable way to experiment with fly fishing before deciding to invest in equipment of your own.

Probably the most precious part of the guided trip is the moment when the guide pulls out his or her own box of flies, and selects the one particular size and color that will get the job done that day. Staring at the array of flies in the arsenal of a professional guide is a hugely educational experience for a novice with a dozen or so standard models kept in a film canister. It is truly an eye-opening moment when one realizes the scope and intensity of the dedicated fly fisher's quest.

This access to hundreds of custom flies, arranged carefully in briefcase-sized fly boxes is just one of the advantages of investing in a guided outing. Some diligent research should produce a reputable shop and guide service in towns close to a fly- fishing river. Try to speak with the guide by phone or, better yet, arrange to meet in person before you decide on a trip. On larger rivers, most guide services offer either walk-and-wade trips, where you drive to a spot and walk in, or drift boat trips, where you spend the day mostly fishing from a rowboat that drifts down the river with the current.

THE BOAT LAUNCH ON THE BIGHORN – SOME ONE-PERSON PONTOON BOATS

The typical style of drift boat is designed specifically for fly fishing; it has a rowing bench in the center and two casting platforms, one fore and one aft. The fly fisher can face in any direction, and can either stand or sit while casting. Whether it is a Mackenzie-style drift boat, made of a fiberglass shell with low sides and a broad bow, or a pontoon drift boat with inflatable rubber pontoons and a steel frame, a guided trip on a drift boat makes for a splendid journey through trout country.

Having a boat easily doubles the amount of river accessible to the fly fisher. These special boats are designed to be easily maneuvered and held in place wherever the fish may be holding, so the guide, and rower, can pick and choose the hot spots on either bank or in the center of the current, allowing you to cast repeatedly and precisely. This vastly increases your odds of catching fish compared to the relatively limited water you can cover by walking and wading.

Drift-boat trips are pricier than the walk-and-wade option, but the experience is unforgettable. The trip will usually last an entire day and cover a long section of water. Drift boats are easy and stable to step in and out of when it is time to access some side channels on foot or stop for lunch.

Fly fishing from a moving boat has its own challenges, such as the simple task of keeping your balance while standing in a moving boat. But it also demands the flexibility of using different techniques to fish different water. A good guide will have several rods rigged up and ready as the character of the water changes. You will get the chance to try fishing with streamers and nymphs, two distinct strategies for catching for fish beneath the surface.

Hiring a guide is money well spent, even for expert fly fishers. It puts you into some good trout water, and gives you some solid advice and instruction. The chance to fish from a drift boat can only enhance the outing further. You'll be left with great memories and knowledge, and a new-found confidence in your skills and ability.

Chapter 15: More Instruction and More Gear

Fly fishing is a billion dollar business. From custom flies mass-produced in Kenya to drift boats and trailers made and sold in Montana, hundreds of companies manufacture thousands of products sold to fly fishers around the world. Rods and reels come in every price range, under dozens of brand names.

The larger outdoor stores have dedicated fly fishing sections. They feature racks of rods, waders and inflatable boats; aisles of flies, boxes and tools; walls of fly-tying material such as hooks, hackle and fur; and glass display cases filled with high-end reels, tying vises and specialty precision tools. For the beginner, the first visit to a large fly fishing store will be daunting but, ultimately, educational. You can now purchase a full fly fishing kit, off the rack in a package, including rod, reel and all your lines, flies and tools, and an instructional DVD for less than $200. The quality may not be top of the line, but you will be set up and casting in no time.

There is also a wealth of information and instruction available in the form of books, e-books, DVDs and, even, YouTube videos – just part of the huge online universe of fly fishing. Classes, courses, small clubs and large organizations exist everywhere to promote and educate new and experienced fly fishers, and most can be found online. Google fly fishing and narrow your search, and you are sure to find an organization or awareness group somewhere close by.

WORKING A STREAM BANK WITH "TROUT UNLIMITED"
BEFORE STOCKING THE STREAM WITH BROOKIES

Joining up with Trout Unlimited, for instance, not only offers exposure to great fishing spots and knowledgeable fly fishers, it adds to your appreciation of the fragile ecosystems that provide the playing grounds for fly fishing.

Through these sites are links to lessons, often through local fly shops. Taking a course in a specific area of fly fishing, such as casting or tying trout flies, will undoubtedly strengthen your skills but, remember, that the cost of a guided trip is probably the best value available in all-around instruction and experience. You can do all of your shopping online as well. Through the Web, you may access all of the research and reviews on a particular type of rod, then shop around for the absolute best price, possibly getting free shipping in the deal.

Always consider the warranty, especially if you are making an investment in a high-quality item. Lifetime warranty should be the rule of thumb once you have decided to spend some real money.

Specialty online catalogs offer countless pages of fly-tying materials, including fur and feathers from birds and mammals you may have never heard of. There are specialty and sub-specialty sites, blogs and forums for every possible angle of the fly fishing culture.

Government or natural-resource websites often publish great information, including stocking reports, which list lakes and rivers that have been stocked for recreational fishing, with dates, numbers and types of fish. The daily flow rate of a particular river, the fishing weather forecast and trend, and the lunar fishing cycles are some of the other facts available online for the inquisitive student.

If you are further inclined, there is also a vast amount of history and background to fly fishing. While some of the classic works are better read in the original book form, volumes of related works can be found on the Internet. These include wild tales of giant fish caught on tiny flies, real-life issues such as watershed management and the damming of rivers, and the growth of industry and its effects on trout waters everywhere. The larger conservation groups monitoring the sensitive corridors from the Yellowstone to the Yukon are constantly publishing new studies on current issues that have an impact on trout ecosystems throughout the region, all available on the Web.

Once fly fishing has captured your curiosity, the sky is the limit. You may invest as much or more time browsing sites and shops or reading fishing guides as you will in actually going fishing.

Chapter 16: Putting It All Together: A Day on the River

This passage is based on real-life experience, and is intended to place you inside a genuine fly fishing scenario. It is loosely set on one of the great fly fishing rivers in North America, the lower Bow River, but can be applied to dozens of rivers in North America. The Bow is born of glacial headwaters high in the Rockies of Banff National Park, and flows eastward, through the city of Calgary and beyond, where it eventually joins the Mississippi. Drift boats are well suited to the wide, flat waters of the Bow. Several guides work the river, for six months of the year, and the fishing is world-class.

It is late August. The mornings are darker but the evenings stay light until well after 8:00. The flow of the river has slowed and stabilized since the runoff, and the water clarity is ideal, or "gin." Water temperatures have hit the median for ideal fish activity, around the 54 degrees Fahrenheit mark. The rainbow trout have grown fat and healthy on a hot summer that followed a rainy spring. They are strong and feisty. Insect life has flourished, both in the water and on the shore. The brown trout will start to spawn in another month or so, but for now they are gorging alongside the rainbows in this wide foothills river east of the Rockies.

DUSK IN AUGUST MEANS THIS WATER WILL SOON COME ALIVE

You have prowled the river and the fly shops this summer. Early mornings and late evenings, in the heat and the rain and the wind, you have been out there, often alone. You have met some fly fishers, shadowy figures who have put in the hours necessary to find fish, learning through experimentation. While fishing on foot, you have seen the drift boats coming, hugging the banks in the distance and coming closer with each cast, the oars turning over slowly, holding the boat in the current.

While walking the river, you have caught some fish and lost some fish, and some days nothing happened at all. The people in the drift boats often catch fish; you can hear the reel screaming as they let the fish run. Then the net comes out and another "big brown" is scooped from the water, flopping heavily as pictures are taken. The drift boats definitely have an advantage, and you are curious.

The phone rings one night and a plan is put in motion. The weather looks fine for the next day and there is one spot in your new friend's boat. Can you make it? You are already packing as you hang up. All next day, dawn to dusk or later, you will have the chance to fly fish from a drift boat, so you had better check the battery on your camera. The pickup arrives at 5:30 a.m.; a boat and trailer are in tow. You toss gear into the box and the adventure begins.

At the boat launch site, in the morning mist, you pull on waders and boots, and then help to slide the boat off the trailer into the river. The truck is parked with keys so that the shuttle service can drive it downriver to the takeout spot. Rods are rigged up as the light of dawn creeps in. The sound of feeding fish can be heard over the rippling water. Some brief instruction follows on how to stand in a drift boat and how not to cross lines with the other caster. You climb in and the rower pushes the boat off into the day. Two fly fishers casting together in a boat requires courtesy and awareness, with the basic rule being "no casting at the same time or at the same spot." One line in the air and one in the water keeps tangles to a minimum. With no obstacles behind, it is easy to lay out long, accurate casts from the drift boat. With a smooth rower on the oars, the boat barely shifts under your feet.

A GUIDED TRIP WILL GIVE YOU THE CHANCE
TO TRY NYMPH FISHING – NOTICE THE BOBBER

It is not long before the first fish is hooked. Your fly goes under in a swirl and the water erupts as you set the hook. It is a much larger fish than you are used to and the rod bows under the sudden strain. The drag is set a little too loose, and as the strong trout makes a run, the reel spins madly, feeding out too much line, which drops in a tangle at your feet. In your momentary distraction, you look down just as the giant fish breaks the water, leaping and twisting in midair only fifteen yards away. It is an awesome rainbow trout, perhaps five pounds and healthy. In your panic you pull instinctively back. Almost in slow motion, the fly pops out of the trout's lip and comes fluttering toward you, while the fish splashes into the river and swims away forever. First fish, two mistakes, no pictures.

- Mistake one – the drag was too loose. Properly setting the drag on your reel calls for planning and feel. It should be loose enough to strip out line and spin, but firm enough to resist the fish's movements. Especially with the better quality reels, which have very precise drag adjustments, it is important to know where the drag is set at all times. Try to experiment with all the drag settings and you'll be ready when the big fish is hooked.
- Mistake Two – the fish jumped and you kept pulling. Always remember to "bow to the king" when the fish jumps, i.e., drop the rod tip and point it at the airborne fish, creating slack in the line. Any tension on the line in the air can easily pull the fly free.

Your buddies in the boat may have more tips for you, so take this opportunity to learn as much as possible. The good news is that a fish saw and liked the fly, so that piece of the puzzle is solved. It is time to dry off the fly and cast again.

The boat floats down the river. More fish are hooked, and you witness experienced fly fishers playing and netting some large rainbow and brown trout. When your chance comes again you are more patient and prepared. You see the fish take the fly and you set the hook firmly to keep it from escaping. It runs and jumps and you keep your cool, while keeping the rod tip high. This time there are pictures of you and your brown trout. Later on, you get a chance to try the oars while everyone gets a chance to fish. It gives you a sense of playing currents and aiming the boat for the target areas where fish may be holding. It also shows how tricky but maneuverable a drift boat actually is.

As the morning passes and the sun heats things up, you pull the boat up to the bank for lunch. Nearby is a small tributary that can be fished on foot. The trees are close by and there is little room to cast. Your buddy is sure the fish are there, so you try a roll cast and a fish attacks your fly but misses it even though you set the hook in time. After waiting a few minutes you cast it again and this time the fish does not miss.

Playing a fish in the close quarters of a small stream means the fish cannot get too far away, so you tighten your drag as the fish begins to fight, and you follow its travels up the stream, using the rod to direct it away from logs or other obstacles.

A crafty fish will often seek out its favorite hiding spot when hooked, and if your line is rubbed against or wrapped around a log in the process, you may lose the fish and the fly. So steering the trout toward open water and smooth shoreline is the best plan. With your buddy helping, the fish is finally netted and released back into the tributary. You have used a new set of skills, based on different conditions. Back in the boat the sun is high and the wind has kicked up slightly.

As you float down river the landscape opens up and the banks become tall and grassy, perfect for grasshopper fishing. Already there have been some violent splashes near the shore as the fish home in on stray hoppers blown into the river by the hot breeze. This makes things easy. With hoppers, casting technique is secondary to simply getting the fly onto the water, then twitching it slightly to make it appear crippled. The fish do the rest, attacking the foam hoppers almost the second they hit the water.

Grasshopper fishing draws out the more aggressive and often larger trout. The fish are big, the fights are challenging, and some fish are lost in the process. It is easy to get snapped off by the mere shake of a head when there is a sizable trout on the hook. You switch to stronger tippets and the matter is resolved.

With grasshoppers on the menu, the fish stay active late into the afternoon, but the landscape has now changed to sloping canyon walls of limestone and shale, with broad stands of cottonwoods lining the flat rocky shoreline below. As a result, there is a shift in the feeding patterns of the fish.

As the sun drops, the mayflies and caddis flies begin to move around and prepare for an evening hatch. In the diminishing light, the fish move up to shallower waters in which it is easier to swim and gorge on the tiny emergers that signal the start of the hatch. The boat is parked and you head out down the shoreline on foot to stalk the shallows. This calls for stealthy movement and careful casting. With the fish schooling up where they are more visible and vulnerable, any disturbance in the water will set them off.

YOU ARE NOT ALONE IN LOOKING FOR RISING FISH

To compound the challenge, you are switching to very small emerger flies which, as the sun sets, are difficult to see against the rippling water. And, mayfly emergers float in the surface film, unlike the upright winged mayfly, which floats on top of the water, so your hands are full with this last challenge of the day.

It is a good time to watch and observe experience in action. Your buddy stands silently by the water's edge, staring into the ebbing light as the purple sky reflects on the current. One sipping trout is feeding in regular rises only ten yards from his feet, then another one appears, and another. You notice mayflies circling up into the trees and floating in the water. A fly lands on you; it is tiny and white. Suddenly, there are millions of them. The fish are rising to the occasion as well.

Your buddy moves like a cat, stripping out line calmly and casting in a whisper, well upstream of where the trout are feeding. He works by sound as much as by sight, timing the drift of the fly into the fish, then watching and hearing the water for any movement as the fly drifts through. One cast, two, three; the suspense is paralyzing. Suddenly he lifts the rod tip, and the calm water explodes in front of him. "Fish on," he says quietly.

You grab the net and follow the action, staying close but out of the way as the fish is guided toward you. Cradling the healthy trout in the net, you consider your next move. You watch it swim away into the shadows, and it strikes you that the light is fading quickly. Fortunately, your fly was tied on in the remaining daylight. You begin casting in the general direction of the last fish. There is no higher test of a fly fisher's skill than casting into the dark and fishing by feel and sound. The fish see your fly, but you see nothing. The fish are there, and you are blindly squinting at phantom waters. You release the fly and it settles, and you listen. You feel a firm tug on the line, and instinctively lift the rod tip; suddenly there's a violent splash and solid pull, followed by a high whizzing of your drag. Fish on!

Even a poor day of fly fishing can be a perfect one. The place, the water, the company, the purity of the sport; there's always something positive and uplifting to take home. You can never know enough about fly fishing. It is a fantastic journey with no real destination, but now you can start the adventure.

About the Expert

Lloyd Bentley won his first essay contest, on fire prevention, at age 9 in San Francisco, California. He wrote for school papers and published a family gossip weekly to entertain the household. He earned a B.A. in Communications in Montreal, and continues to hone his craft, seeking out new challenges that feed his passion and test his skill. During the course of 20 years in Banff, Alberta, Canada, he became both a writer and adventure junkie. He attended a writer's workshop at the Banff Centre, scripted radio drama for Parks Canada, and contributed Web articles on hiking and biking. He also tells a great fishing story.

HowExpert publishes quick 'how to' guides on all topics from A to Z by everyday experts. Visit HowExpert.com to learn more.

Recommended Resources

- HowExpert.com – Quick 'How To' Guides on All Topics from A to Z by Everyday Experts.
- HowExpert.com/free – Free HowExpert Email Newsletter.
- HowExpert.com/books – HowExpert Books
- HowExpert.com/courses – HowExpert Courses
- HowExpert.com/clothing – HowExpert Clothing
- HowExpert.com/membership – HowExpert Membership Site
- HowExpert.com/affiliates – HowExpert Affiliate Program
- HowExpert.com/writers – Write About Your #1 Passion/Knowledge/Expertise & Become a HowExpert Author.
- HowExpert.com/resources – Additional HowExpert Recommended Resources
- YouTube.com/HowExpert – Subscribe to HowExpert YouTube.
- Instagram.com/HowExpert – Follow HowExpert on Instagram.
- Facebook.com/HowExpert – Follow HowExpert on Facebook.